I AM NOT A NUMBER

Written by Jenny Kay Dupuis *and* Kathy Kacer
Illustrated by Gillian Newland

Second Story Press

The dark figure, backlit by the sun, filled the doorway of our home on Nipissing Reserve Number 10.

"I'm here for the children," the shadowy giant said, pointing a long finger at me. "You! How old?"

I shrank behind my mother. *Here for the children?*

"How old?" he repeated.

"Eight." The whisper floated from my mouth.

The Indian agent marched into our house and approached my father. "You knew I would come, Ernest," he said. "The children are going with me to the residential school. They are wards of the government, now. They belong to us."

"Not Irene! She needs to be with her family." My mother wrapped her arms around me. "I won't let you take her."

The man shrugged. "Give me all three or you'll be fined or sent to jail."

"We have no choice, Mary Ann," my father replied, sounding defeated. "It was only a matter of time before they came for the children."

Fear rose inside me, filling my throat. My brothers George and Ephraim stood with their heads bowed low. *Are they as scared as I am?* I wondered. My other brothers and sisters, those too old and too young to be taken, huddled together, watching.

My father pulled my two brothers and me into a semicircle before him. "This man will take you to live in a school far from here," he said in his soft, calm voice. "We don't want to let you go, but it's the law; we have to."

"But why are you letting him take us?" I cried, pulling away. Father's hands trembled and tears pooled in his eyes. My loving father – chief of the community, strong and wise – turned away without answering.

"Hurry up!" The Indian agent was becoming impatient.

My mother gathered food into three small packets. "Something for their journey," she explained as the Indian agent tapped his watch.

"Mom?" I asked. "Are you coming with us?"

She shook her head.

"But who will look after me?" I cried.

"There will be teachers – and nuns," my mother said. "You will learn many things at this school." Something in her voice – a quiver, a hesitation – made me doubt that this was true. My dread turned to panic.

"I don't want to leave you," I whispered.

My mother pulled me up against her, and I buried my face in the folds of her dress, pressing her tighter until there was no air between us. I couldn't let go.

The Indian agent opened the door and motioned for us to come. Mom pried my arms from around her back and kissed the top of my head. I grabbed the back of George's jacket and stumbled after him as he stepped toward the door. At least I had my brothers with me. I made a silent vow that we would stay together.

As we walked into the sunlight toward the waiting bus, my mother ran forward. "Look after each other," she cried. "Never forget home or our ways. Never forget us. Never forget who you are!"

I turned one last time and gazed at her through blurry tears. *How could I possibly forget my parents? How could I forget who I was?*

But then, how could I possibly guess what awaited me at the residential school?

"Girls, follow me. Boys, you will be going to a separate building."
A tall nun named Sister Mary stood at the entrance of the
imposing brick building. My heart sank into my stomach as the
boys were led away. No chance for good-byes. The tiny spark of
safety I had felt in being with my brothers flickered and died.
I turned back to face Sister Mary, feeling more alone than ever.

"My name is Irene Couchie," I told her. My voice was small,
but I held my head high and clasped my hands together so that
no one could see they were shaking.

Sister Mary's eyes narrowed to slits. "We don't use names
here. All students are known by numbers. You are 759."

*I am not a number. I am Irene Couchie, daughter of Ernest
and Mary Ann Couchie. I will never forget who I am.*

I was hurried to the showers with the other girls who had arrived with me. We stood in a group as icy water pricked our bodies. Sister Mary hovered over us. "Make sure to scrub all the brown off."

"She must like lighter-skinned girls better," someone next to me whispered.

I stared at my dark arms while Sister Mary scrubbed them with foul-smelling soap. After I was dry, she handed me a plain gray dress, knitted stockings, and a pair of black leather shoes. Dressed in my new uniform, I was taken to a small room and ordered to sit on a low stool. The worst was still to come.

Sister Mary wrapped a cape around my neck. "Now, let's get rid of that hair. Sit up straight," she ordered.

Her scissors chewed through my long, black hair, and I watched my locks fall in a pool around me. This meant much more to me than a haircut, though I could never explain that to Sister Mary. Back home, long hair was a source of pride. We cut it when we lost a loved one. Now it felt as if a part of me was dying with every strand that fell.

Several days later, I sat with the other girls at a long wooden table, staring at the bowl of porridge in front of me. It was gray and lumpy and looked like the plaster my father had once used to fill some cracks in our wall. Next to the porridge was a piece of stale white bread. I thought of my mom's freshly baked loaves and homemade strawberry-rhubarb jam. Back home, we had never had much, but we were never hungry. Here, my stomach gurgled, calling out for food.

"Eat!" Sister Mary's stern voice cut into my thoughts. I forced some bitter, gritty mush down my throat. The smell nearly made me gag. But I remembered the warnings of the other girls. *If you don't eat your meal at breakfast, they will serve it to you for lunch. And if you throw it up, you will have to eat the vomit.* I raised spoonful after spoonful to my mouth and willed myself to keep it down.

"I'm so hungry," the girl opposite me groaned.

I broke off a piece of the bread and leaned across the table. "Here," I said. "I don't want this."

She smiled and reached for it gratefully. "Miigwetch."

"Miigwetch gayegiin," I whispered back.

I didn't see Sister Mary until she was almost on top of me. *Thwack!* A big wooden spoon came down hard across my shoulders. I yelped in pain.

"That's the devil's language!" she shouted. "We don't speak it here." She grabbed my arm and hauled me up the stairs. Sister Mary's strides were long and fast and I stumbled behind her, trying not to fall. I had seen other girls pulled along like this. *Lessons.* That's what the sisters called it when one of us needed reminding about the rules. I was terrified of what awaited me in the room at the end of the hallway.

Sister Mary shoved me into a chair and turned away to fill a bedpan with hot coals from the stove.

"Show me your hands," she said.

"Please don't hurt me," I whispered.

"Show me!" she demanded.

There was no escape. Slowly, I extended my arms straight out as Sister Mary lowered the hot bedpan onto my skin. I wanted to scream. Instead I dug my teeth into my lower lip and squeezed my eyes shut as tightly as I could, counting the seconds until the sister lifted the pan.

"That'll teach you to speak English here. You should be ashamed of yourself!" With that, she walked away.

I blew gently on the red welts that had bloomed down my arms. *Ashamed?* I wasn't ashamed of my language. I was proud of it. But everything I knew and loved about who I was and where I had come from was slowly being taken away. Mother's last words – *Never forget who you are* – rang in my ears. "I'm Irene Couchie. I'm trying to remember," I whispered, as tears streamed down my face.

A couple of weeks later, I was in the chapel for early mass as I was every morning and twice on Sundays. "If you memorize the songs and pray a lot, you will go to heaven," the sisters told us. I didn't mind chapel. It was better than hauling firewood to feed the school's hungry furnace, or mending worn clothes that were piled in the sewing room. Sister Elizabeth sat next to me and squeezed my hand. She was kinder than most of the nuns. Once, she gave me a piece of juicy steak and leftover potato when I was helping clear away the hearty meal that the sisters and teachers had eaten.

I returned her smile and then searched the pews on the other side of the chapel, trying to find Ephraim and George. Because boys and girls were separated, chapel was the only place where I could see them.

Ephraim looked my way. He was pale. *Are you okay?* I raised my eyes, silently asking the question. He nodded slightly and then leaned forward in his seat as if he were asking about me. I closed my eyes in response. My arms were still tender, and even though the red sores had now turned pink, the memory of the punishment had not faded one bit.

I knelt on the pew, troubled. *Why are we treated so cruelly? Why must I change everything about myself?* While I sang the songs and prayed out loud, I secretly begged God to let me return to my family.

Days, weeks, and months limped along drearier than a never-
ending storm. Up at 6:00 a.m., prayers, porridge, chores,
studies. But the gloom of each day was better than the fear of
punishment.

I dreamed of being back on the reserve, where I could play
with my brothers, sisters, and cousins. I wanted to hear the song
of the meadowlarks in the grasslands. I yearned to spread my
arms wide, as if I were ready to soar, like them. I longed to fly
away, but for me there was no escape.

Just as I was beginning to believe that my time at the school would never end, an announcement was made that lifted my spirit. We were going home for the summer! *Home!* I hadn't said that word for so long. Would my house look the same? Would my parents know me? I had not heard from them all year; hadn't been allowed to write or receive letters.

"It's evil out there," Sister Mary told us. "We can't have you mixing with the outside world."

But everyone knew the nuns were afraid that our families would learn how we were being treated.

When I saw my parents standing in front of our house, I knew that home was as it had always been. Mother rushed to greet us and nearly pulled me off my feet as she wrapped her arms around me. My father squeezed my cheeks. "I've thought about you every day," he whispered.

"I never forgot you," I replied. "I never forgot who I am."

Dad smiled and bent his forehead to touch mine.

That evening we sat down to a feast of meat pies and fried pickerel. Wanting us to take as much as food as we liked, mother urged us on saying "Gidaan, gidaan."

I piled extra fish onto my plate, realizing that I had not heard my Ojibway language spoken in nearly a year. "Miigwetch," I replied. The words I knew so well felt strange in my mouth.

But at night, when I put my head upon my pillow, I was haunted by images of Sister Mary chasing me down a long hallway with a leather strap in her hand. I bolted awake and tried to stop my heart from pounding. Finally, I got out of bed and sat by the open window, where the familiar sound of water lapping up on the lakeshore calmed my breathing.

But the nightmares did not end there. I knew that all too quickly, the leaves would turn from green to bright red and orange, signaling the time when the living nightmare of that horrible place would be upon me.

"Don't make me go back. Please!" I pleaded with my parents. I had slowly begun to tell them what had happened to us at the school. Dad's eyes darkened when I talked about Sister Mary's "lessons," and Mom covered her ears and could not bear to listen.

"I need to find a way to keep you here," my father said. "We must have a plan."

I clenched my hands into tight fists. *Yes! We need a plan! But what?*

"But if we disobey, what will they do to us?" Mom asked.

"Let them do what they want," Dad said. "We won't send our children back to that place. We'll hide them – make sure the Indian agent can't find them."

We all started to talk at once. We could hide upstairs in the bedrooms. But the Indian agent would search every corner to find us. We could hide behind the house. But we would be easily spotted back there. We could run to the lake and hide among the reeds. But no, they were not thick enough to conceal us. Then Dad suggested something.

"You could hide in my shop."

My father had a taxidermy shop on our land that was close enough to run to, yet separate from the house. *Will it work?* I wondered. *Will my father's shop give us the protection we need?* I looked at my brothers and at my parents. We nodded our heads in quiet agreement – a silent pact. We had a plan. And the summer was slipping away.

When the dreaded day arrived, I was in the yard helping Mom hang laundry. The wind blew my hair around my face. My hair was growing. Soon, it would reach down my back.

"He's coming!" My older sister's shout cut through the air.

I dropped the laundry basket and peered around the corner of the house. There he was – my kidnapper.

The same Indian agent who had taken me away a year earlier was marching up the road, one determined step after another.

Mom froze in place, looking as frightened as I felt. Then my father ran out the back door with Ephraim and George just ahead of him.

"Irene!" He grabbed my shoulders. "You and the boys go and hide in the shop."

My feet would not move. "Don't let him take me away," I begged.

"Run!" my father ordered. He turned me around and shoved me forward.

I tripped and then regained my footing. We had a plan, and it was time to put it into action. My brothers were sprinting across the property, and I set off too. We ran for our lives until we reached the shop, pushed the door open, and tumbled inside.

"Hide!" I shouted.

We dove behind some large crates, settling in where we wouldn't be seen. From where I hid, I could see through a window to the outside. Before long, I spied the Indian agent striding up the path with my father close behind. I placed my finger across my lips to warn George and Ephraim to be quiet. Then the door creaked open.

"I know you're in here." I remembered the voice of the Indian agent. Sweat trickled down my back.

"I sent the children to stay with family farther north." It was my father's voice. "Don't know when they'll be back."

I moved my head ever so slightly to try and see what was happening. The Indian agent, feet apart, arms crossed, was staring at my father. "You'd better not be lying, Ernest," he snarled. "You'll be in a lot of trouble if you don't send your kids back to the school."

Then my loving father – chief of the community, strong and wise – raised himself up to his full height. "Do whatever you want," he replied in a voice that was low and even. "Call the police. Have me arrested. You will NEVER. TAKE MY CHILDREN. AWAY. AGAIN!"

Seconds that felt like forever passed. My father stared at the Indian agent, and the agent glared back at him. I held my breath. Would the agent leave? Would we be discovered? I glanced over at Ephraim and George. Their eyes had grown wider than full moons.

A lifetime. An eternity. Then, without another word, the Indian agent turned and left the shop.

For a while, no one moved, uncertain that the danger had passed. But when my father slowly turned and stretched his arms wide, the three of us tumbled from our hiding places and flung ourselves into his embrace. I was laughing and crying at the same time and shaking from head to toe. We were safe. I was Irene Couchie, daughter of Ernest and Mary Ann Couchie.

And I was home.

The Residential School System

Irene Couchie Dupuis was among approximately 150,000 First Nations, Métis, and Inuit children – some as young as four – who, for over a century, were removed from their homes and sent to live at residential schools across Canada. The schools were created and funded by the federal government in the belief that Indigenous peoples were uncivilized and needed to be "saved" from themselves. In reality, that "education" cost Indigenous children the loss of their families and communities, their Indigenous languages, and their traditions.

The schools were run by Roman Catholic, Presbyterian, United, and Anglican churches and were staffed by nuns, priests, and teachers. Rules were strict, conditions harsh. Children were poorly fed; infectious diseases thrived; many students died alone and far from home. Basic skills and trades were taught, but generally children were overworked, and the quality of education was poor. Those who broke the rules were punished. Most of the children felt lonely, isolated, and unloved.

Of the over 80,000 students who either returned home or relocated to cities and towns across Canada, many felt they didn't belong anywhere and struggled all their lives. Some survivors suffered intense shame over what they endured as children. Others, without having been raised by their parents, had difficulty raising their own children. Still others continue to feel the impact of residential schools on their lives to this day. The last residential school closed in 1996.

Under the watchful eye of their teacher, solemn residential schoolgirls have their photo taken in a class very much like the one Irene attended.

In 1986, The United Church of Canada apologized to the Indigenous peoples for their experiences in residential schools. Since then, former students have sought recognition and compensation. Not until 2008 did the Prime Minister of Canada issue a statement of apology.

In 2015, the Truth and Reconciliation Commission released its final report. After listening to thousands of survivors, their families, and communities, the Commission acknowledged the extent of the impact and suffering that residential schools caused. It took great courage for former students to come forward and share their stories. The goal of the report, which included 94 calls to action, was to honor the truth and to try to establish a more positive relationship between Indigenous peoples and non-Indigenous Canadians, one that respects the diversity of First Nations, Métis, and Inuit communities.

There are still many difficult stories like Irene's waiting to be shared. Each one reminds us that the residential school system was devastating and, quite simply, wrong. Before we can heal as a nation and before Indigenous peoples fully regain their pride and sense of belonging, there is still much work to be done.

Afterword by Jenny Kay Dupuis

I Am Not a Number is based on the true story of my granny, Irene Couchie Dupuis, an Anishinaabe woman who was born into a First Nation community that stretched along the shores of Lake Nipissing in Northern Ontario. Granny's father was chief of the community, and her mother looked after their fourteen children. The Couchie house was modest, with no electricity or running water. Everyone

Some of the Couchie children. George is at far left, Ephraim is beside him. Irene stands at far right, and their mother, Mary Ann, is seated behind them.

Irene's father and my great-grandfather, Chief Ernest Couchie.

helped with daily chores. They didn't have a lot of material goods, but they valued family, and that was more important than almost anything else.

In 1928, when Irene was still a young girl, she and her two brothers were taken from their community of Nipissing First Nation to live at Spanish Indian Residential School. While she was a student there, Irene suffered neglect and abuse. She and the others were regularly strapped or shamed for not following the many harsh school rules. The children were not permitted any regular contact with their parents. Their names were replaced by numbers. My granny's number was 759.

After a year of suffering in these terrible conditions, Irene was finally allowed to go home for the summer. When her father learned what had happened to her at the school, he hid her and her siblings so they wouldn't be found when the Indian agent returned. She never went back to that place.

My granny rarely spoke about her year away, but when I was a teenager, I wanted to learn more about the legacy of the residential school system and understand what she and many others had endured. Stories about the residential school system were seldom told in our community, but Granny told me hers. I felt it was important. All of the stories – told and untold – are important. They are part of our history, and they still affect many people today. This is why I wanted to share my granny's – Irene Couchie Dupuis' – name and her truth with you.

My granny, Irene Couchie Dupuis.

For my late grandmother and all the Indigenous children who endured the Indian Residential School System. With special gratitude to my relative Les Couchi for his genuine, unending support.
—Jenny Kay Dupuis

For Gabi and Jake, with love as always
—Kathy Kacer

Acknowledgments:
Special thanks to Margie and the staff of Second Story Press for creating an inclusive space and always believing in me; Kathy for her expertise, guidance and kindness; Gillian for her stunning illustrations that respectfully reflect my grandmother's life experiences; my family for trusting me to share the memories. —J.K.D.

So many people to thank: Margie and the staff of SSP for their ongoing commitment to bringing these important stories to young readers; the Canada Council for the Arts for their financial support; Gillian for the perfect illustrations; Jenny for sharing her important family story and for trusting me to help her tell it. —K.K.

Text copyright © 2016 by Jenny Kay Dupuis and Kathy Kacer
Illustrations copyright © 2016 by Gillian Newland

Photo on page 30: Canada. Dept. Indian and Northern Affairs/
Library and Archives Canada/e011080274

Editor: Kathryn Cole
Designer: Melissa Kaita

Printed and bound in China

Second Story Press gratefully acknowledges the support of the Ontario Arts Council, the Ontario Media Development Corporation, and the Canada Council for the Arts for our publishing program. We acknowledge the financial support of the Government of Canada through the Canada Book Fund.

Published by
SECOND STORY PRESS
20 Maud Street, Suite 401
Toronto, ON
M5V 2M5
www.secondstorypress.ca